Flexibility, Enhanced Cooperation and the Treaty of Amsterdam

Flexibility, Enhanced Cooperation and the Treaty of Amsterdam

Kerstin Junge

KOGAN PAGE

First published in 1999

Kogan Page Limited
120 Pentonville Road
London N1 9JN

Web site: www.kogan-page.co.uk

Concise yet comprehensive, the Dossiers present accessible analysis of EU policies, institutions and related themes. Written by experts in the field and commissioned by the London European Research Centre of the University of North London, the European Dossiers are an invaluable source of information and interpretations for anyone with an interest in the EU.

Published five times per year, the Dossiers are available through an annual subscription or as individual titles.

Comments on the series or proposals for new titles are welcome in writing to the series editor:

Professor Michael Newman
London European Research Centre
University of North London
166–220, Holloway Road
London N7 8DB

British Library Cataloguing in Publication Data

ISBN 0 7494 3023 0

Typeset by JS Typesetting, Wellingborough, Northants.
Printed and bound in Great Britain by Selwood Printing Limited.

Contents

Biographical Notes vii

Editorial Board viii

Acknowledgements ix

1. Introduction 1

2. The Interdependence of Deepening and Widening in the Process of European Integration 5

The historical dimension of deepening and widening 5

Obstacles to deepening and widening in the late 1990s 10

3. The Dilemma between Deepening and Widening in the late 1990s and Possible Solutions 23

4. The Debate on Differentiated Integration in the Context of the 1996 IGC and the Flexibility Clause of the Treaty of Amsterdam 43

The political debate on differentiated integration 44

The flexibility clause of the Treaty of Amsterdam 49

5. Summary and Conclusion 57

References 61

Bibliography 65

Appendix: Abbreviations 73

Biographical Notes

Kerstin Junge is a PhD student at the University of Birmingham researching the area of differentiated integration. She studied European Studies at the Universities of Osnabrück and North London.

European Dossier Series: Editorial Board

Acknowledgements

I would like to thank Mike Newman, Mike Smith and an anonymous referee for their helpful comments on content and style of earlier drafts of this Dossier. I am also grateful to Peter Gowan for encouraging this publication.

1

Introduction

After each enlargement and in times of stagnation of the European integration process alternatives to the predominant mode of uniform integration have been sought by both academics and politicians. That intra-Community heterogeneity is an obstacle to the deepening of the European integration process was acknowledged for the first time in the 1970s. At this time Willy Brandt, then leader of the German social democratic party (SPD), and the then Belgian Prime Minister Leo Tindemans proposed a two-speed strategy for the introduction of economic and monetary union and European Community (EC) Commissioner Dahrendorf promoted the introduction of Europe *à la carte*. When, in the 1980s, the prospect of the southern enlargements made at least the economic differences between the member states more obvious, the debate about differentiated approaches to an 'ever closer union' gained momentum again. In the 1990s, after the adoption of the Maastricht Treaty and the prospect of further enlargement, the Community faces a crisis once more. The substantial deepening agreed to at the 1991 Intergovernmental Conference leading to the adoption of the Maastricht Treaty in combination with the prospect of an eastern enlargement reveals clearly the changing character of the EC and the limits of uniform integration. Parallel to the challenges of deepening and widening in the 1990s the capability of alternative, differentiated, strategies of integration to solve these problems is discussed intensively once more.

This Dossier attempts to contribute to the discussion about differentiated integration by examining why the predominant mode of uniform integration is likely to become increasingly impractical in an EU15+, by considering the alternative strategies of differentiated integration discussed before and during the 1996 Intergovernmental Conference, and by looking at possible scenarios for the future.

In the first chapter the relation between deepening and widening of the EU will be analysed. On the basis of the interdependence of the two tasks in the past we will show that the situation of the Community in the 1990s is qualitatively different: both the challenge of deepening posed by the Maastricht Treaty and the prospect of enlargement will demand changes in the traditional method of integration. Although the list of applicants also includes countries from southern Europe, the discussion will concentrate on eastern Europe: not only do these countries form the largest group of potential new EU members but, for various reasons, their accession will also be more difficult than that of other countries.

In the second chapter, therefore, the six major concepts of differentiated integration will be introduced. These are multi-speed Europe, Europe of concentric circles, core Europe, flexible integration, Europe *à la carte* and variable geometry. An examination of their exact content is necessary in order to avoid misunderstandings as to their meaning and implications. If existent, examples of their use in the current EU will be given for further clarification. The order in which the concepts are discussed corresponds to the *finalité politique* they promote: concepts that promote supranationalism are discussed at the beginning, those whose adoption would reduce the EU to an intergovernmental organisation are examined later.

After a brief discussion of member state attitudes towards these concepts of differentiated integration, the third chapter discusses the flexibility clauses in the Treaty of Amsterdam. We will show that, because of the many restrictions to its application, the main asset of the respective provisions is the fact that they have been introduced into the Treaty at all.

In the conclusion, finally, we will summarise the main arguments presented in the Dossier and address some possible scenarios for the future.

2

The Interdependence of Deepening and Widening in the Process of European Integration

THE HISTORICAL DIMENSION OF DEEPENING AND WIDENING

The tasks of deepening and widening have occupied the European Community throughout its existence and indeed have developed a symbiotic relationship with each other in the course of the past decades. The process of deepening, ie the communitarisation of policies and the extension of competencies of the supranational institutions, takes place both on the intergovernmental and supranational levels of the EU. The direction in which the European integration process is heading, and the necessary changes to the Treaties, are decided by the European Council at intergovernmental conferences (IGCs). Of the three IGCs held to date (1985, 1990 and 1996), the first two were particularly influential in terms of the process of deepening. The core project of the 1986 Single European Act (SEA) was to realise the Common Market. To that end, the SEA introduced not only the necessary provisions to realise the four freedoms (free movement of labour, goods, capital and services) but also institutional reform. In order to facilitate its introduction, qualified majority voting in the Council of Ministers was introduced for most areas related to the Single Market. The introduction of the cooperation procedure gave the European Parliament (EP) more power in the decision-making process. The Maastricht Treaty on European Union (TEU) introduced the project of creating a European Union. This included not only the aim of Economic and Monetary Union (EMU), which will have important direct and indirect implications for deepening, but also provisions on closer cooperation in justice and home affairs and foreign and security policies (albeit on an intergovernmental level). The TEU also continued with institutional reform by further extending the powers of the EP as well as qualified majority voting in the Council.

While thus on the intergovernmental level decisions regarding the basic framework of the development of the Union are taken, the supranational institutions (Commission and European Court of Justice) play a decisive role in shaping the implementation of these decisions. In the past, both institutions have managed to develop the European integration process (sometimes) beyond the original intentions of the member states. Cram (1994) points out that the Commission exerts an important influence on the EU policy-making process. As a bureaucracy ultimately concerned with extending its scope of competence, the Commission has 'learned to respond to opportunities for action as they present themselves, and even to facilitate the emergence of these opportunities' (Cram 1994 p199). For instance, through the preparation of non-binding reports, opinions and programmes (eg in the social policy field) or cooperation with industry (in the case of IT policy), the Commission has frequently laid the basis for more binding initiatives at a later time when the member states were more likely to accept the initiatives. The European Court of Justice (ECJ), on the other hand, has a crucial role in both constitution building and policy making. In a series of cases in the 1960s the Court has gradually established the principles of direct effect and supremacy of EC law over national law (constitution building), thus 'fundamentally altering the legal character of the Community from that negotiated by the member states' (Wincott 1995 p588).

> *'Direct effect' is the idea that Community law, as such, creates rights within the legal systems of the member states. In consequence, individuals could use Community law rights in national courts, even if those rights had not been implemented (or had been adequately implemented) into domestic law by the national legislature (Wincott 1995 p588).*

These two principles, together with Article 177 of the Treaty on the European Community (TEC), which allows national courts to transfer matters of interpretation of Community law to the ECJ, constitute the basis for the ECJ's role in policy making. Its hitherto pro-integrationist interpretation of EU law has not only enforced the actual application of existing provisions but has also laid the foundation for the creation of new policies.

These two levels of policy making in the EU mean that deepening is a continuous process that is not restricted to decisions taken at the IGCs. However, for the relation between deepening and widening, IGCs are of particular importance since only on this level can the reforms required by widening be adopted.

Not only has the Community been deepened continuously, it has also taken in new members throughout its existence, never having understood itself as a closed club. Article 237 of the Treaty of Rome stated that 'any European State may apply to become a member', a formulation that is also found in Article O of the TEU. Indeed, the Community has attracted non-members since the very beginning, and functions increasingly as a magnet in Europe. Until now, three waves of enlargement have increased the number of member states from the original 6 to 15. In 1972 Britain, Ireland and Denmark joined the

European Community. The Mediterranean enlargements of 1981 and 1986 made Greece, Spain and Portugal member states. In 1995 the first enlargement of the European Union brought the three EFTA countries – Austria, Finland and Sweden – into the Union. In addition, the 1990s have added to these past accessions a long list of applicants from southern and eastern Europe. Thirteen countries have submitted their application for membership in the past ten years: the Mediterranean countries Turkey (1987), Cyprus and Malta (1990); the Visegrad countries Poland and Hungary (1994), Slovakia (1995) and the Czech Republic (1996); and the remaining east Europeans Bulgaria, Rumania, Estonia, Latvia, Lithuania (all 1995), and Slovenia (1996). In November 1997 accession negotiations between the Community and the six most advanced applicant countries (the Czech Republic, Hungary, Poland, Estonia, Slovenia and Cyprus) started. Their accession will increase the number of EU member states to 21.

Preston (1995) finds that over the past decades a 'classical Community method of enlargement' has evolved that consists of five key principles. They are 'derived from a number of explicit and implicit assumptions about the rights and duties of both existing members and applicant states' (Preston 1995 p452) and include the following elements:

1. Applicants accept the *acquis communautaire* in full. No permanent opt outs are available.
2. Formal accession negotiations focus solely on the practicalities of the applicants taking on the *acquis*.
3. Problems created by increasing the economic diversity of an enlarged Community are addressed by the creation of new policy instruments overlaid on existing ones rather than by fundamental reform of the inadequacies of the latter.
4. New members are integrated into the Community's institutional structure on the basis of limited incre-

mental adaptation, facilitated by the promise of a more fundamental review after enlargement.

5. The Community prefers to negotiate with groups of states that already have close relations with each other.

It is easily observed that this method encumbers the acceding countries with the bulk of adjustment, while to date the Community has had to make only superficial changes to its system. Nevertheless, it is more than mere coincidence that the IGCs of the 1980s and early 1990s coincided with two waves of enlargement. As Pinder (1992) points out, both the Mediterranean enlargement and the unification of Germany were one motive for deepening through the SEA and the TEU. The SEA laid down not only an increased use of majority voting but also the requirement of the EP's assent to future associations and accessions. After the unification of Germany 'both France and Germany wanted to ensure that the Community would remain a strong and stable framework within which to anchor the larger and more powerful Germany' (Pinder 1992 p415). Economic and monetary union as well as first steps towards political union in the form of increased power for the EP and the establishment of the second and third pillars were to serve this aim.

While in the past decades the member states were able to enlarge the Community without jeopardising the aim of creating an ever closer union, the inherent tension between the two tasks has become obvious in the Maastricht Treaty. The TEU was the first visible sign that the heterogeneity of attitudes on the character of the EU, brought about by continuous enlargement, is an obstacle to deepening. Increasingly, however, enlargement will not only become a political problem but also a numerical and economic one. The following section will explore the internal and external obstacles to deepening the Union in the late 1990s and argue that the present situation is qualitatively different from past decades.

OBSTACLES TO DEEPENING AND WIDENING IN THE LATE 1990s

The internal situation

Past enlargements have added to the original six member states countries with differing historical backgrounds and political traditions. Accordingly, the diversity of views on and ideas about the nature of European integration and its goals began to vary greatly and the dichotomy between federalists/europhiles and intergovernmentalists/eurosceptics evolved and consolidated. Indeed, this heterogeneity is one of the major obstacles to a uniform progression of all member states towards an 'ever closer union'. While some countries, which on the whole agree with a federal goal of European integration, have proved to be mostly supportive of deepening, those that prefer intergovernmental cooperation have been much more resistant towards the transfer of national sovereignty to the supranational level.

The founders of the Community shared a high degree of commitment to European integration and the federal *finalité* of the EU. This europhile attitude is based on a unique combination of idealistic and functionalist motives for European integration that originated in their special experience of the Second World War and that have complemented each other throughout the post-war period. Influenced by the federal movement, the French and German founding fathers of the Community emphasised the necessity to create a European federation in order to secure peace on the continent by providing a framework for Franco-German reconciliation and transferring certain national core competencies to a supranational authority. However, this project was only successful because all six countries, each in a specific way, predominantly gained from supranationalism, politically and economically. Although national interests did and do prevent an unconditional adherence to the goal of an 'ever closer union', the history of European integration, in the course of which the Franco-German axis has developed into the motor of European integration, is proof that the commitment of the original six members to a unified Europe is stronger and more comprehensive than that of the later members.

This group of 'deepeners' has subsequently been joined by countries that, due to their different historic experiences (especially of the Second World War) and political traditions, are much more sceptical towards supranationalism and would like to see the EU as a mere free trade area. Already the first enlargement brought two of the persistently most eurosceptic countries into the EC that continued to put much emphasis on the protection of their national sovereignty. Britain and Denmark lack the idealistic background of the founding countries and entered primarily out of economic calculus: they feared the economic disadvantages of staying outside the Community. Both countries regarded the EC as a free trade area, a view that was certainly not disproved by the state of the EC at the time of their accession and that is still influential today. Both Britain and Denmark have continuously rejected plans to create a supranational political union, not only concrete initiatives such as the 1981 Genscher Columbo initiative or the intergovernmental conference to negotiate the SEA, but also developments that were suspected of indirectly leading to political union, such as EMU or (in the case of Britain) social policy. The recent opt outs from some core provisions of the TEU confirm the prediction that Britain and Denmark will remain reluctant members.

With the accession of Sweden and Finland in 1995 two more countries with an essentially intergovernmentalist tradition and strong emphasis on national independence, originating in their special geographic position, entered the Union. As Miles (1995 p327) says: 'Their membership applications are not the result of a conversion to a federal Europe but rather the culmination of domestic and international trends that make wider Nordic EU membership a political and economic necessity'. Economic recession and rising unemployment since the early 1990s made EC membership more attractive to the Scandinavians than it appeared before: it was to support the liberalisation of their economies. As with the Danish and British applications the main motives for Swedish and Finnish membership were overwhelmingly pragmatic. It can thus be assumed that moves towards supranationalism will be complicated further, not least because the accession of two more countries with strong intergovernmental traditions has changed the numerical balance between federalists and confederalists in favour of the latter. It should be noted, however, that the current Finnish government seems to have adopted a pro-European position. This is, *inter alia*, exemplified by its decision to join EMU. Furthermore the countries' strong democratic tradition is also very likely to be an obstacle to their full participation in justice and home affairs (JHA). On the other hand Finland and Sweden are expected to put much weight on the development of the social and environmental policies so that progress in these areas has become more likely.

The applications for membership of the southern Europeans (Greece, Portugal and Spain) was primarily politically motivated. All three countries had only just become democracies and membership was to secure social and political stability. Despite their late membership and worse economic preconditions, at least 'the Spaniards and the Portuguese have become rather more whole-hearted Europeans than the British' (Bideleux 1996 p127) and support the EU's federal goal. However, as a result of their weak economies, their support for European federalism tends to manifest itself in demands to strengthen intra-Community cohesion (ie transfer payments from 'North' to 'South') in connection with deepening efforts. Thus, the policies of the south Europeans play an ambiguous role regarding the effects of these on the federal/confederal outcome of European integration. On the one hand transfer payments are indeed an integral part of a federation, and their claims contribute to the development of federal structures in the Union; on the other hand by linking deepening to an increase in transfer payments they could become at least as great obstacles in this process as countries with an intergovernmentalist tradition, since the net contributors to the EU budget are increasingly reluctant to raise their contributions.

As the last paragraph indicates, past enlargements have increased not only the political heterogeneity but also the economic disparities of the EU. The first and second waves of enlargement have added to the original, economically relatively homogeneous, member states countries with different economic structures and lesser wealth. As a result, the economic geography of the present EU is characterised by a centre–periphery dichotomy. The centre of the EU, ie the six founding countries and Austria, represents the region of economic growth, interdependence and technological innovation in Europe (often also referred to as 'blue banana'). Its character as the EU economic powerhouse also finds its expression in the gross domestic product (GDP) and unemployment figures of the region. In 1995 the centre had a GDP per capita of well above the EU average, while the levels of member states at the European periphery were below or just above the Community average (Europäische Kommission 1997 p153). The same trend can be found in the unemployment figures. In 1994 the level of unemployment in the centre was around the EU average of 10.7 per cent. In the periphery, however, unemployment was between 14 and 22 per cent (Britain and Greece excluded) (Eurostat 1996 p8).

Of the peripheral member states, the economies of especially the Mediterranean countries are structurally weak and can still be characterised by relative underdevelopment due to late and partial industrialisation. While Ireland started off under similar conditions in the 1970s and still has the second largest agricultural sector in the Community (after Greece), it succeeded in modernising its industry and lifting its GDP to 93 per cent of the Community average (Europäische Kommission 1997 p153). The economies of Portugal and Spain, however, still rely heavily on labour-intensive, low-technology methods of production in areas such as textiles and building. In Portugal, for instance, advanced technology and capital-intensive products (metallurgy, chemicals, engineering, electrical and transport equipment) only accounted for around 10 per cent of the GDP in 1989 (da Silva Lopes (ed) 1993 p70). According to Holman (1996 p151):

> *in comparative terms Spanish industry is characterized by a high labour/capital ratio and a low competitive power* vis-à-vis *its counterparts in the highly developed member states; a concentration of manufacturing activities in low growth industries; an import dependence on investment goods and foreign technology; and a progressive export orientation on labour intensive products and natural resources.*

The south Europeans thus remain more rural and technologically backward than the north European countries, which makes them sensitive to competition from outside and hinders their economic development.

The Treaties of Maastricht and Amsterdam are, in many respects, a product of this political and economic heterogeneity of the EU member states. The TEU lays the foundation for comprehensive deepening of the Union and the eventual establishment of a political union. With the creation of EMU on 1 January 1999, 11 member states have irrevocably fixed the exchange rates of their currencies and handed over responsibility for their monetary policy to the European Central Bank. EMU participants have thus lost control over decisive economic instruments, hitherto understood as integral parts of national sovereignty. Some argue, however, that EMU will *de facto* increase economic sovereignty of the other participating countries because they will cease to be unilaterally dependent on the German Bundesbank. It is also widely agreed that eventually the economic and fiscal policies of EMU participants will have to be harmonised in order to ensure a smooth functioning of EMU. EMU itself as well as potential spillovers has thus the potential to take the EU a quantum leap forward towards a quasi-federal system. The TEU thus gives an important direct and indirect impetus to the creation of a closer union between the participants. Indeed, EMU is often seen as a vehicle to bring about political union (PU), a goal that seems nearly impossible to achieve otherwise. In the TEU, for instance, the provisions on PU were left outside the EC framework and moved into two intergovernmental pillars. However, they are regarded as having 'potentially far-reaching implications' (Nugent 1992 p320). The agreements on a common foreign and security policy (CFSP), the second pillar of the EU, do not only comprise coordination of all aspects of a foreign and security policy but also offer the prospect of a common defence policy. In the third pillar JHA decisions taken, for instance, on asylum and immigration are seen as a precursor for respective Community activities.

The Treaty of Amsterdam does not dissolve the pillar structure of the EU. However, the Treaty communitarises most issues of the third pillar (such as border controls, asylum, immigration and visa policy, prevention of and fight against crime) and the Schengen agreement by moving them into the first, 'supranational', pillar of the EU. This means that after a transition period of five years following the adoption of the Treaty the Community institutions will be involved in the decision making: majority voting in the Council will become possible and the Commission will gain the full power of initiative. Only cooperation of police and justice will still be covered by the third pillar. The provisions on the CFSP, although not as far-reaching as those on JHA, also have clear deepening implications. The Treaty of Amsterdam introduces the explicit aim to create a common defence policy, encourages intensive EU–WEU (West European Union) relations and anticipates an eventual integration of the latter in the EU. The objective to make the WEU the instrument of a Common Defence Policy is further pursued with the integration of the so-called Petersberg tasks of the WEU into the Treaty.

However, both Treaties also express the growing discrepancy between the objectives of deepening and widening. The Maastricht Treaty could only be adopted due to the application of strategies of differentiated integration and the introduction of a three-pillar structure. The more sceptical member states, Britain and Denmark, were permitted to opt out of EMU (Britain and Denmark) and the social protocol (Britain). Due to the great economic heterogeneity of the EU some member states considered it necessary to introduce convergence criteria that institutionalised multi-speed Europe. At the same time the creation of the intergovernmental second and third pillars for CFSP and JHA respectively must not only be judged as an attempt by the member states to withdraw these issues from the influence of the Community institutions, but can certainly also be interpreted as a compromise solution to bring into accord diverging attitudes on the issue of political union. Deepening in order to, *inter alia,* link the enlarged Germany firmly in the Community thus had to be paid for with an increase in the complexity of the Community structure.

While at Maastricht differentiation of integration was agreed on only reluctantly and regarded as an exemption, the Treaty of Amsterdam for the first time in the history of European integration includes a recognition of the potential obstacles of enlargement to deepening. Section V *Closer Cooperation – 'Flexibility'* permits a majority of member states to 'establish closer cooperation between them' provided that the *acquis communautaire* as well as Community policies, actions or programmes are not affected. With this clause the abandonment of the convention to progress in unison towards an 'ever closer union' (Preamble of the TEU) is sanctioned. After the ratification of the Treaty by all member states this clause will enable certain countries to continue with the deepening of policy areas where persistent resistance by their partners would otherwise prevent progress. The application of flexible integration might thus even contribute to accelerating the deepening of certain policies if member states that originally were not interested in their development do not want to stay behind.

While the aim of the 1996 IGC was to review the Maastricht Treaty the prospect of an eastern enlargement was certainly also considered in the process of drafting.

The external situation

After the accession of the three EFTA countries Austria, Finland and Sweden in 1995 enlargement still remains on the political agenda of the EU. As has been mentioned above, at present 13 countries have applied to become EU members. We are thus faced with the paradoxical situation that, in a period of relatively low enthusiasm for European integration in the EU member states, to non-members it seems to be more attractive than ever. This phenomenon can be attributed to two factors. First, the Community has been extraordinarily successful in economic terms over the past decades. The implementation of the Single Market, induced by the 1986 SEA, as well as the settlements on EMU and political cooperation in the Maastricht Treaty, *de facto* established the EU as the economic and political centre in Europe. Consequently European non-member states are in a situation of one-sided dependence: in order to be able to gain access to EU markets they have to obey EU norms and standards but lack the possibility of influencing their creation. At present only full EU membership solves this predicament as the present alternatives (European Economic Area (EEA) and association agreements) exclude countries from EU decision making. Second, the fall of Communism in eastern Europe induced the transition process to liberal democratic systems and market economies. The east European countries thus started to fulfil the essential preconditions for application for EU membership. However, their inclusion will have a particularly great impact on the Union. Apart from the number of applicants from the region there are political and economic reasons why an eastern enlargement will provoke difficulties.

The reasons for the 'drive towards the West' of the central and east European countries (CEEC) are to a quite decisive extent of a psychological and political nature. For many eastern Europeans EU membership symbolises their return to Europe, a definite break with their former Communist system and Russian hegemony. At the same time they see the EU as a guarantor of inner political and social stability. The threefold transformation process (from command to market economy, from authoritarianism to democracy, from centralism to decentralism (Timmermann 1993 p714)) has created insecurities thus far unknown to the people in eastern Europe. The political orientation towards the EU, which is regarded as a symbol of political stability and economic wealth, and the explicit aim of a fast accession are to create the popular consensus that will prevent a halt in, or a revision of, the transformation process. It provides the basis and justification for (unpopular) reforms and austerity programmes by offering an attractive perspective for the future. In compliance with these motivations the CEEC governments are pursuing europhile policies and demanding a fast inclusion of their countries in the EU. Also, a vast majority of the populations approve of accession to the EU. In Slovakia and Hungary, for instance, surveys constantly reveal that 70–75 per cent and 80 per cent of the populations respectively are in favour of EU accession (Samson 1996 p133; Borsámyi et al. 1996 p151). However, certain characteristics of the debate on accession to the EU in the CEEC indicate that they might not be easy partners for the present member states after all.

Moorhouse (1996 pp368–9) points out that, in the Visegrad countries, the political and economic consequences of EU membership are, even at the level of political elites, not discussed exhaustively. There is a tendency to overemphasise the advantages of accession while little debate on key issues of European integration takes place. Even among political elites there is thus only slight awareness about the real implications of EU membership. The reasons for this phenomenon must, above all, be sought in the still rather centralised structure of the political systems of the CEEC. Unlike in western democracies, participation of non-political actors (such as experts, lobbyists and the media) in decision shaping is too low to be able to really affect the governments. Instead, only a few high-profile politicians exert a great personal influence in the formation of policies. Consequently potentially valuable sources of information are lost and the strategies of the CEEC towards the EU tend to be based on incomplete and simplified information (Moorhouse 1996 pp368–9).

The centralism of post-Communist political systems also means that there is a great potential for discontinuity. The personalisation of the CEEC European policies means that leadership struggles and electoral defeats can provoke sudden policy swings. This danger is consolidated by the fact that the aim of EU membership is by no means uncontroversial between different political parties. In the Visegrad countries, for instance, there is a split between the bourgeois parties of the centre (centre-right and centre-left) that approve of integration into western structures, and the nationalist and post-Communist parties that object to the western orientation of their governments (Samson 1996 pp85–139).

Even more than in the EU15, the interest in European integration in the CEEC is restricted to political and intellectual elites. Examining attitudes towards the EU in Hungary in the years 1992–3, Maczonkai finds that those with a university or college degree and the politically active are more supportive of the EU than others. Generally, the populations are less informed than the (political) elites about possible consequences of EU membership and current problems of European integration.

Moreover, there is also a clear social split in the expected benefits of accession to the EU. While the political and intellectual elites tend to have rather idealistic reasons to approve of EU membership, the populations in the CEEC have very concrete expectations of EU membership. In Poland and Hungary, for example, rising living standards and more modern technology are the two major gains expected from EU membership by the population. In Hungary for example, 77.4 per cent of the population expected more modern technology, and 48.8 per cent a rise in the living standard from EU membership (Borsámyi et al 1996 p153). For Poland see Holzer (1996 p97). The combination of incomplete information about potential costs of membership on the one hand and the lack of solid ideological foundations for euro-enthusiasm on the other constitutes a possible source of difficulties. If expectations and realities clash, and EU membership reveals the full scale of adaption required, the euro-enthusiasm of the populations can easily change into euro-pessimism and will also affect the European policies of the CEEC governments.

The CEEC will not only bring a distinctive political background into the EU but also an economic situation that is very different from that of the present member states. The Commission acknowledges in Agenda 2000 that all CEEC have made considerable progress in the transition to market economies and indeed characterises five CEEC as functioning market economies (the Czech Republic, Estonia, Hungary, Poland and Slovenia). However, in the first years of the transition process all CEEC experienced a dramatic decline in output: 'cumulative falls in GDP (at constant prices) between 1989 and 1993 ranged from 16 per cent in Poland to 79 per cent in Lithuania' (Grabbe and Hughes 1997 p18). Only in 1998 has the region returned to growth, and only Poland, Slovenia and the Czech Republic are expected to reach a GDP level higher than in 1989 this year (*Financial Times* 1998). The

CEEC are thus still much poorer than the present EU member states. The GDP in purchasing power standards (in ecu per inhabitant) of the CEEC10 in 1995 was only 32 per cent of the EU15 average. All CEEC were worse off than Portugal and Spain, the poorest EU member states at present. With an average of 42 per cent of the EU15 average Hungary, Poland, Estonia, the Czech Republic and Slovenia are slightly richer. The Czech Republic and Slovenia even reach 55 and 59 per cent of the Community average respectively (Europäische Kommission 1997 p153).

The CEEC are not only much poorer but also more agricultural than the EU15. The share of agricultural production as a percentage of the GDP of the ten CEEC applicants was three and a half times higher than the EU15 average (8.6 compared to 2.4 per cent). The data for the five CEEC likely to enter the EU first are only slightly better, with agriculture constituting 6.4 per cent of the GDP. With 22.5 per cent of the work-force employed in agriculture, the CEEC10 exceed the EU15 level by the factor 4. Again there are slightly better figures for the Czech Republic, Hungary, Poland, Slovenia and Estonia (12.3 versus 5.4). In Poland, however, more than a quarter of the work-force (26.9 per cent) are employed in the agricultural sector (Europäische Kommission 1997 p153). As '[f]or most CEECs, a rapid decline in the size of the agricultural sector would cause urbanization and unemployment on a scale transition economies could not cope with' (Grabbe and Hughes 1997 p42), drastic restructuring before their accession seems unlikely.

With the CEEC10, countries would thus join the EU whose economic structure is, and will for some time remain, very different from that of the present member states. The eastern enlargement will thus contribute not only politically but also economically to an increase in intra-EU heterogeneity and make the process of deepening more complicated. Indeed, one important element of the European policy of the CEEC that has already become apparent, and that will continue to be important, is a certain reluctance to transfer sovereignty to another political bloc (Moorhouse 1996 p370). It will thus generally, but also in particular, become more difficult to continue with the political deepening of the EU. On a general level the greater heterogeneity will make it more difficult for member states to agree on the direction of the integration process. In particular, however, it will paralyse the Council of Ministers unless voting procedures are reformed.

3

The Dilemma between Deepening and Widening in the late 1990s and Possible Solutions

The situation of the EU in the late 1990s is thus qualitatively different from previous deepening–widening situations.

On the one hand the Community has become much more integrated since the adoption of the SEA than it was before. In particular, the realisation of EMU on 1 January 1999 is likely to move the EU a quantum leap forward towards supranationalism.

Never before, on the other hand, have more countries applied for EU membership and have prospective member states been politically and economically as unstable as the CEEC.

The consequences for the European integration process are twofold. First, the classical Community method of enlargement will, at least partly, become impractical. The EU, instead of merely imposing the burden of adjustment on the CEEC, will actually have to adapt to enlargement itself by introducing major reforms of policies and institutions. This necessity was recognised at the Copenhagen European Council, which made '[t]he Union's capacity to absorb new members, while maintaining the momentum of European integration' one of the accession criteria for the CEEC. Because the CEEC are so poor and agricultural, a simple extension of the structural funds and the common agricultural policy (CAP) would bankrupt the EU budget. Estimates of the additional costs of extending the structural funds to the CEEC10 range from 14 to 38 billion ecu, figures for the CAP vary between 12 and 38 billion ecu for inclusion of the CEEC10 and the Visegrad countries respectively (Grabbe and Hughes 1997 pp40–4). With member states increasingly concerned about their contributions to the EU budget, such a dramatic increase in its size is unlikely. Instead, both policies will have to be reformed, which will mean that both the 'old poor' and the 'new poor' member states will receive less financial aid from the Community than in comparable situations in the past.

Furthermore, a comprehensive overhaul of the institutions will become compulsory. Accession of ten or more countries to the EU will dramatically increase the number of Commissioners, members of the European Parliament (MEPs) and members of the Council, and risk paralysing the respective institutions.

In both cases the eastern enlargement will enforce reforms that have been recognised as urgent for a long time but that were impossible to carry out due to the resistance of the poor or small member states and the agricultural lobby.

Second, full membership of the CEEC will make the deepening of European policies more difficult than it is today. In the environmental policy, for instance, the gap between EU standards and those in the CEEC is particularly wide. Moreover, costly adaptation to EU standards is regarded as a luxury and a dangerous regression into protectionism by some east European governments (Moorhouse 1996 p375). In social policy the gap between EU standards (eg in the workplace) and CEEC laws is equally wide. Due to the connected costs it will take a long time to reduce, as both policies tend to obstruct the transformation to capitalism. As intergovernmentalist and neo-liberal currents have a great influence on the CEEC governments they are likely to object to a further deepening of those policies. This is equally true of reform of the CAP and the regional policy. As the CEEC will become major beneficiaries of those policies once they are full members it seems likely that they will reject changes to their detriment. While reform of those policies is difficult at present, after the next enlargement it will become nearly impossible. Problems will also increase for the CFSP. Already it is extremely difficult, if not impossible, for member states to reach a common viewpoint on foreign policy matters, as the EU's reaction to the Yugoslavia crisis has shown quite clearly. The inclusion of the CEEC will increase the diversity of national interest: the goal of a *common* foreign and security (and defence) policy that establishes the EU as a political actor on the international platform will become even more difficult than it is at present.

In view of this increasingly tense relation between deepening and widening, three general strategies can be adopted in order to be able to carry out both tasks.

1. *Deepening first:* in order to maintain the governability of the Union substantial institutional and policy reforms are carried out before new member states are accepted. Agreement of all member states to a federal *finalité politique* and the creation of 'efficient, effective, and democratic institutions' (Wessels 1993 p28), that are able to implement the respective policies are prerequisites of widening.
2. *Widening first:* the east European countries are included quickly in the EU in order to secure their economic and political stability. The Union in its present shape is a product of the cold war and constitutes neither a natural unit nor an optimal area for the solution of all problems. The fall of Communism offers the chance to overcome the artificial exclusion of east-central European countries from Europe.
3. *Parallel widening and deepening:* both tasks can and should be pursued at the same time. Every applicant

state that fulfils the accession criteria must be accepted and rapid reforms of institutions and policies carried out. To that end a differentiation of integration is necessary in order to account for both the increasing political and economic heterogeneity of a widened Community.

While in the past the first strategy prevailed, parallel widening and deepening seems to be the strategy of the future. 'Deepening first' is becoming increasingly impractical as the balance between federalists and intergovernmentalists has shifted in favour of the latter, which reinforces a pragmatic approach towards European integration. Deepening first also risks postponing enlargement indefinitely by blocking EU institutions and governments with difficult negotiations of deepening, further raising the access level for potential member states and solving the problem of increased heterogeneity of the member states unsatisfactorily. 'Widening first', on the other hand, would indeed endanger the European integration process by provoking a dramatic increase of heterogeneity and straining the Community budget. Ignoring the necessity of deepening could thus further a decline of the EU into a free trade area.

At present, therefore, 'parallel deepening and widening' seems to be the only viable strategy, as it takes into account the importance of both tasks as well as the intra-Community obstacles to their realisation.

Consequently, in the years preceding Maastricht II and at the 1996 Intergovernmental Conference itself political and academic circles discussed the question of how best to combine the tasks of eastern enlargement and reform of the EU. In autumn 1994 Schäuble, Lamers, Balladur and Major put forward proposals on how to implement the provisions agreed to in the Maastricht Treaty while at the same time preparing the EU for enlargement. With their papers they 'put flexibility on the agenda of the IGC' (Stubb 1997 p42). The subsequent years saw a fast expansion of the discussion, with an ever increasing number of proposals being put forward. Although academics started to define and categorise the various concepts the debate on differentiated integration is still characterised by a confusion about the exact meaning of individual concepts. In particular, the terms multi-speed Europe, variable geometry and Europe *à la carte* are used in very different contexts, thus obscuring differences between them. In the following section we will therefore introduce the six most common concepts of differentiated integration in order to expose their unique characteristics. This will be done by beginning with the most integrationist concept (multi-speed Europe) and finishing with the least integrationist one (variable geometry).

Multi-speed Europe

The idea of multi-speed Europe – also referred to as two-speed, two-/multi-tier Europe or graduated integration – was introduced in 1974 in the speech of Willy Brandt at the *Organisation Française du Mouvement Européen* in Paris (Brandt 1975). One year later it was taken up by Leo Tindemans in his 1975 Report on the European Union (Commission of the European Communities 1976). Its development is closely related to the plans of the 1970s to introduce economic and monetary union. While mostly evoking negative reactions in the 1970s, the debate on differentiated integration in the context of the 1996 IGC showed that multi-speed Europe had become widely accepted by heads of state and government as one strategy to cope with increasing heterogeneity in the EU (see below).

Both Brandt and Tindemans assumed that the goals of integration, the *finalité politique* and *economique*, are accepted and achieved by all member states. Both authors recognised, however, that *objective* (ie economic) differences between member states can make it impossible for them to move in unison towards the agreed goals (and particularly towards economic and monetary union).

Consequently, Brandt and Tindemans suggested that those countries that are able and willing to progress should be allowed to do so. Tindemans even argued that they had 'the duty to forge ahead'(Commission of the European Communities 1976 p20) in order to strengthen the Community. The countries whose objective situation does not allow a fast progression are allowed to stay behind temporarily and advance in accordance with their abilities. This, however, does not mean a permanent separation of the vanguard from the rearguard: the slower countries must be supported by the more advanced countries in order to facilitate the catching-up process. Subsequently, multi-speed Europe was used in a wider sense. Originally restricted to economic integration, it is now also referred to in the context of political integration.

Multi-speed Europe is thus essentially a supranational approach. By assuming that all member states of the EU are able to agree on common goals it presupposes a potential for the creation of an 'ever closer union' in Europe and seeks to overcome the technical barriers to this process. 'Graduated integration can only work profitably if there is a broad underlying consensus' (Langeheine and Weinstock 1984 p191). The concept is thus more strongly committed to the idea of a supranational Union than any other concept of differentiated integration.

Multi-speed Europe focuses primarily on *time* and is thus closely related to the transition periods often granted to new member states. However, unlike accession treaties, in which 'the stages along the road are determined in advance and are binding on all Member States' (Langeheine and Weinstock 1984 p187), multi-speed Europe does not force members to obey a set timetable but allows each country to accommodate the pace of its progress to its specific (economic) situation. The aim is not to achieve permanently differing levels of integration, as promoted by the idea of Europe *à la carte*. Since the goal of integration is commonly agreed the member states maintain the same policies and actions, not simultaneously, but at different times. The levels of integration remain therefore only temporarily different. 'If one Member State stops before reaching the goal it is not integration at a different speed we are looking at, but integration in a different way'.[1] Consequently, and in contrast with a Europe *à la carte*, the slower countries are permitted to participate fully in both the negotiations and voting on the respective policies.

Examples of multi-speed Europe can already be found in the present Community. The TEU explicitly permits the development of a two-speed Europe in connection with EMU. Those countries that fulfil the convergence criteria are allowed to participate from the start and thus represent the vanguard. The 'rearguard' of economically less developed countries will join EMU later.

Other articles of the TEU also allow for integration at multiple speeds. These are, *inter alia*, article 7c (exemptions on the completion of the common market), 115 (shifts in trade flows) and 130t (additional measures taken by the member states regarding the protection of the environment). All of them try to take into account differences in the economic structures of the member states and allow for graduated integration.

The European Monetary System (EMS) is a classical example: all member states supported its creation although some, 'primarily for objective reasons' (Langeheine and Weinstock 1984 p193), did not participate from the beginning (Britain and Greece); provisions were made that allowed the 'laggards' to participate in discussions on the functioning and the development of the EMS.

Concentric circles

Concentric circles seems to play a greater role in the academic debate on differentiated integration than in the political debate. In 1994, for instance, R. E. Baldwin, in

[1] 'Integration at Multiple Speeds in the European Union', http://www.nxn.net/home/ernst/eu1.htm, p1

his book *Towards an Integrated Europe*, attempted to reconcile the tasks of deepening and widening by developing a model of concentric circles.

Generally, the approach comprises the idea of dividing Europe into several concentric layers, or circles: around a smallest central layer two or three other layers are arranged. These circles increase in size the further away they are from the centre. The geometric result of this approach thus resembles a wedding cake, looked at from above.

The intensity of supranational integration increases from the largest bottom circle of very low integration to the top circle with the highest degree of unification. Accordingly, the number of countries taking part in the respective circles decreases from the bottom to the top layer. However, membership in one circle is not permanent and 'upward' mobility is possible as soon as the necessary economic conditions are fulfilled and a political will for further integration exists. Each member of one of the smaller circles is also a member of the wider circle(s).

Concentric circles is based on a 'predetermined view of the geographical organisation of Europe' (Langeheine and Weinstock 1984 p188). It focuses on countries and their different economic and political abilities to participate in European integration. The general assumption is that the further away from central western Europe countries are, the less able or willing they are to take part in EU activities.

In Baldwin's model, the EU with all of its member states forms the top layer of the 'wedding cake' and thus the circle of deepest integration. The middle circle consists of countries in an intermediate phase, similar to the EEA. It constitutes a quasi-forecourt for EU membership: the members of the middle circle have close economic and political relations to the EU, but do not participate in all the policies of the first layer and have only a limited influence in the decision-making process. The middle circle contains those CEEC that have strong enough economies to withstand the competitive pressures of a shared market with EU countries and that do not greatly strain the Union's budget. The third and largest layer, finally, includes countries that are linked to the EU merely via association agreements and are thus prospective member states. Today's bilateral Europe Agreements would be regionalised so that not only EU–CEEC trade would be liberalised but also intra-CEEC trade.

However, Baldwin's proposal is not the only imaginable variant of concentric circles. The geographical result of core Europe (see below), for instance, is one of concentric circles, too. In this case the top layer consists of the founding countries of the Community (according to the German proposal without Italy) that are closely linked in political, economic and military terms; this core will possibly develop into a federal state. The medium layer would comprise those member states who favour at least trade liberalisation; it would thus be politically less binding than the top circle and be a mere free trade area. The bottom circle would consist of those non-EU member states with whom the Union would establish diplomatic, security, economic or commercial links. These could include both the remaining members of the EEA and advanced CEEC.

Even today's organisation of Europe could be described as one of concentric circles. The EU is the central circle of closest integration, the EEA represents the middle layer and the CEEC that are linked to the EU via Europe Agreements make up the bottom circle.

Regarded superficially, concentric circles is a geographical approach as it focuses on countries and groups of countries. However, the actual composition of the various circles is not primarily determined by the geographic situation of a country in Europe, but by its ability and willingness to take on the obligations of membership of the respective circle. This, however, exposes concentric circles as a merely descriptive approach: it describes the geographical result of integration according to other paradigms. Baldwin's approach, for instance, shows great similarities with multi-speed Europe, while other proposals show a striking similarity with core Europe. Unlike the other concepts, concentric circles can thus not be regarded as an independent approach towards European integration.

Core Europe

The idea of a European core, grouped around the Franco-German axis, has been described by Scharrer (1984 p16) as a 'constant of French European policy'. Mentioned first by de Gaulle (Stercken 1969 pp250–1), the idea was taken up again in 1994 by the then French Prime Minister Edouard Balladur in an interview with the daily newspaper *Le Figaro* on 30 August. Only a few day later, on 1 September, the parliamentary faction of the German Christian-Democratic Union (CDU)/Christian-Social Union (CSU) under the leadership of Wolfgang Schäuble and Karl Lamers presented their position paper 'Reflections on European policy' (see also Lamers 1997). Both proposals summed up French and German positions on flexibility on the eve of the 1996 IGC. In 1995 Christian Deubner published his examination of core Europe, entitled *Deutsche Europapolitik: Von Maastricht nach Kerneuropa?*

The basic idea of core Europe, as expounded by Balladur and Schäuble *et al.*, is that a small number of EU member states that are able and willing to – the core – proceed faster than the rest with the task of deepening the Union in order to prevent it from disintegrating. The Franco-German cooperation will have to assume a leading role in this process. In Balladur's proposal the task of the core is above all to implement EMU and to create a European defence union.

Schäuble *et al.*, however, take the idea one step further. In their opinion the core would constitute, and have the task to be, a strong centre in a large and heterogeneous Union that would prevent the EU from falling apart. Members of the core must thus 'not only participate ... in all policy fields, but [they] should also be recognisably more Community-spirited in their joint action than others' (Lamers 1997 p109). The core is not meant to be a 'closed club', an end in itself, but must be open to every member state that accepts its 'rules'. Ideally it functions as a magnet and attracts those countries that originally were not willing or able to participate in further integration. In the long run the core would thus make itself superfluous. Consequently, core Europe is conceived as a temporary means to pursue the tasks of deepening and widening simultaneously.

Controversially Schäuble *et al.* determine membership of the core only indirectly according to functional criteria. They assume that a core of five to six 'europhile' countries already exists at present (the founding countries Germany, France and the Benelux countries; Italy is not mentioned), but refrain from explaining this composition. Deubner's only functional criteria for the selection of core countries are their ability and willingness to participate in EMU. His other criteria for determining members of the core are predominantly historical and cultural. On the basis of various surveys, studies and reports on such matters as European identity, cultural and religious ties he reaches the same conclusion about the composition of the core as Lamers and Schäuble. Thus, in contrast to the variable geometry approach, the core does not form because certain countries by coincidence share the same interests. In the Schäuble/Deubner concepts the core forms naturally because the participants are culturally, politically and economically more homogeneous than the other member states and thus quasi-automatically share the same interests.

Core Europe is in essence a supranational approach. It aims at maximising integration by establishing the hard core as a vanguard of countries that among themselves develop deeper integration. The separation of core and periphery is not meant to be permanent: ideally both circles merge into one eventually. Unlike multi-speed Europe, core Europe does not assume that the goal of integration is commonly agreed to from the beginning. Instead it acknowledges the increasing political heterogeneity of the EU by permitting a homogeneous core of countries to deepen controversial policy areas. Regarded superficially, core Europe is thus a geographic concept as it focuses on countries. Since, however, the core is open to each country that agrees with its rules it is in fact a functional concept.

Examples for core Europe do not exist at present. It could be argued, however, that in the near future those countries that participate in EMU and are part of the Schengen agreement form a quasi-core of the EU. On a more theoretical level core Europe could also be the result of a Europe of variable geometry or multi-speed Europe. In the first case, the core would consist of those countries which are at the point of intersection of all policies and participate in all policy areas. In the latter it would be made up of the more advanced countries progressing faster towards the agreed goal.

Europe *à la carte*

The idea of Europe *à la carte* was first introduced by former Commissioner Ralf Dahrendorf in 1979 in his Jean Monnet lecture 'A Third Europe?' in which he introduced the following definition: 'Europe *à la carte*, that is common policies where there are common interests without any constraint on those who cannot, at a given point of time, join them' (Scharrer 1984 p13). It is also a concept long associated with representing the British approach towards European integration. Margaret Thatcher, in her 1988 Bruges speech, identified as one guiding principle for the future of the Community that '(w)illing and active co-operation between independent sovereign states is the best way to build a successful European Community'. Both John Major's Leiden speech in 1994 and the British White Paper 'A Partnership of Nations. The British Approach to the European Union Intergovernmental Conference 1996' have also been interpreted as promoting a Europe *à la carte* as the future paradigm for European integration (Stubb 1991 pp41–2; Giering 1997 pp79–80; Ehlerman 1998 p5).

As the epithet *à la carte* expresses, this concept of European integration is compared to a menu: every member state is allowed to pick and choose the policy areas (and thus the degree of integration) in which it is interested and that it is willing to pursue.

In the political and academic debate Europe *à la carte* is used in two variants. Some understand it as a form of integration where member states of the European Union agree on a minimum set of common goals, participation in which is compulsory, but permit opt outs of, or rather non-participation in, any policies that are not part of this lowest common denominator.[2] 'Picking and choosing' would thus be realised in all fields of integration in all three pillars of the EU that do not form part of the common basis. Others regard Europe *à la carte* as a mode of integration that is subject to no rules at all: each European policy is available for picking and choosing. A lowest common denominator on which all member states have to agree would not exist. For representatives of this line of thought see, for example, Langeheine and Weinstock 1984 p187; Centre for Economic Policy Research (CEPR) 1995 pp52–3; Giering 1997 p75.

Both variants have in common that they focus on national interests and take into consideration the growing reluctance of member states to transfer sovereignty to the EU level. Thus regarding the increasing social, political and economic heterogeneity of the EU as an insurmountable obstacle to the creation of an ever closer union, Europe *à la carte* promotes a shift away from uniform progression towards a supranational, increasingly federal, political system. Instead, the concept moves the EU in the direction of a purely intergovernmentalist organisation. Due to its focus on policies Europe *à la carte* is a functional approach.

Despite the broad rejection of this mode of integration, aspects of a Europe *à la carte* can be found in today's

[2] The concept is used in this meaning by, eg Dahrendorf (see Scharrer 1984 p13); Ehlermann 1998 p6; Stubb 1997 p39.

Union. The most prominent examples certainly are the TEU provisions permitting a British and Danish opt out of the third stage of EMU. The provisions allow both countries to abstain from EMU even if they fulfil the convergence criteria. Another example was Britain's refusal to sign the social charter in 1989 and her opt out of the TEU protocol on social policy. Until 1997, when Tony Blair signed the protocol, Britain was not allowed to participate either in the negotiations or in the voting of the Council on matters relating to social policy covered by the protocol.

Further examples of aspects of Europe *à la carte* in the present EU are Denmark's opt outs from a (prospective) common defence policy and its interpretation of citizenship. According to the 'Declarations regarding Denmark' of the TEU, Denmark is not obliged to join the WEU and will not participate in the preparations and the execution of decisions and measures of the EU related to defence (section C). Section A states that the TEU provisions on citizenship of the Union do not replace national (regulations on) citizenship. A less prominent example is the provision on second homes in Denmark, which permits the country to keep its legal provisions on the purchase of second homes regardless of the provisions laid down in the TEU (first protocol of the TEU).

Flexible integration

Unlike most of the other concepts, flexible integration is a new approach. It was developed in 1995 by a multinational team of academics of the London-based Centre for Economic Policy Research. Flexible integration was introduced as a contribution to the discussion on deepening and widening before the 1996 Intergovernmental Conference.

The main characteristic of flexible integration is its dual structure. The approach consists of a *common base*, a set of policies that has to be accepted and agreed upon by every member state, and *open partnerships*, policies outside the common base, integration of which is optional.

The common base is created in order to prevent the EU from disintegrating:

> *The common base contains all those policy areas over which integration is deemed indispensable for all members: it is the minimum requirement for participation in the EU and, at the same time, the largest common denominator of the Union (CEPR 1995 p58).*

The academics of the CEPR determine three policies that should be included in the common base: the Single Market (in order to preserve the four freedoms) and the common agricultural and regional policies (in order to facilitate enlargement politically and support the economic recovery of the CEEC). As the common base is well defined and relatively narrow, the member states are more likely to agree to transferring more sovereignty to the supranational institutions so that the democratic deficit might be able to be reduced.

The open partnerships can be organised in two ways. Either only one open partnership per policy area is allowed or several open partnerships in the same policy are permitted. 'An example may be three environmental open partnerships to protect the water quality of the Mediterranean, the Baltic Sea and the North Sea respectively' (CEPR 1995 p61). In order to prevent discrimination and ensure that the new partnerships remain open, all EU members must participate in setting up the partnership; the entry rules must be agreed to at the beginning of the formation of the partnership. The open partnerships are administered in an intergovernmental fashion.

Although these two forms of cooperation would exist separately from each other, the possibility exists of integrating the policies of the open partnerships into the common base.

Due to its emphasis on policies, flexible integration is a functional approach that focuses on the political and economic heterogeneity of the member states. The concept shows a strong similarity with the first variant of Europe *à la carte*. Although flexible integration is phrased more positively than Europe *à la carte* – the opting *out* of policies becomes an opting *in* – the basic idea behind both concepts is similar. On the basis of a lowest common denominator member states are permitted to choose those policies whose integration is interesting and functional for them. The result in both cases is different levels of integration as a final, not temporary, outcome.

The arrangements of the TEU on EMU are an example of flexible integration in the present EU. All member states participated in creating the respective provisions, the entry rules were determined by all member states in advance and every country that fulfils the convergence criteria is allowed to join. In decisive difference to a system of flexible integration, however, Britain's and Denmark's opt outs were granted only on an exceptional basis.

Variable geometry

The concept of variable geometry was first introduced in 1979 by Gérard Tardy,[3] a member of the French *Commissariat Général du Plan*. One year later, it was used by the *Commissariat* itself (1980) as well as by Jacques Delors.[4] As with Europe *à la carte*, it can describe two phenomena.

First, variable geometry can be understood as a 'mode [of integration] that admits to unattainable differences within the integrative structure by allowing permanent or irreversible separation between a core of countries and lesser developed integrative structures' (Ehlerman 1998 p5; used in this sense also by CEPR 1995 pp56–8, Chaltiel 1995; Giering 1997 p76). Understood in this sense variable geometry can presume the existence of a compulsory basis for common policies. This basis can be supplemented by

[3] At a conference of the Trans European Political Studies Association (TEPSA) in Scheveningen on 18–19 June 1979.

[4] Agence Europe, No. 3037, 10 December 1980.

additional and varying forms and degrees of (intergovernmental) cooperation in other policy areas. Different member states would be members of different circles of cooperation. A Europe integrated according to variable geometry understood in this sense would presumably have as its centre the common market (possibly with some flanking policies) and, arranged around this centre and overlapping with it, and with each other, several subcentres representing different forms of intergovernmental cooperation. In a strict sense this variant of variable geometry is a collective term for concepts such as Europe *à la carte*, core Europe and variable geometry.

In its second meaning variable geometry envisages a Europe of polycentric circles without a common centre. It thus ceases to regard the existence of a lowest common denominator as basis for a European Union as compulsory and aims at including the whole continent, thus renouncing the member state/non-member state dichotomy. Accordingly, and in a much more radical way than the concept of Europe *à la carte*, this approach is functional in the sense that proponents of this strategy see European countries integrated exclusively according to the most efficient way to solve their particular economic and political problems. In practice, for instance, this could mean including present EFTA-members in economic and monetary union in order to create an optimal currency area, but excluding the economically more backward southern member states.

A Europe of variable geometry understood in this second meaning would result in a disintegration of the EU as we know it today. Europe would turn into a confederation and a free trade area at the most: in an area of multiple functional circles with varying membership the current institutional and legal framework of the EU would become superfluous. This variant of variable geometry is thus the most radical (and negative) approach of all the models attempting to solve the problem of deepening and widening. Adopting this paradigm for European integration would mean giving in completely to the idea of insurmountable national interests. It would mean regarding and accepting the mode of European integration pursued until today as a failed experiment.

In accordance with this radical approach towards European integration examples of variable geometry are rare and restricted to areas outside the common EU framework. These are areas of industrial and research cooperation on certain projects between different, but not all, member states and third countries. Eureka and the European Bank for Reconstruction and Development (EBRD) are two classical examples of this. Members of Eureka, the European initiative to strengthen European competitiveness in research and technology, include, in addition to the EU member states and the Commission, the EFTA countries, Turkey and Hungary. The largest shareholders of the EBRD, which supports private and entrepreneurial initiatives contributing to the transition of east European countries to market economies are, apart from the EC (member states and European Investment Bank), the USA, Japan and the target countries themselves. Prominent examples of variable geometry between EU member states are: the cooperation of French, German, British and Spanish aircraft industries on the airbus; the Franco-German-Belgian eurocorps; and the Schengen agreement, which was originally agreed by France, Germany and the Benelux countries and has subsequently been joined by Italy, Greece, Portugal and Spain and is included in the first pillar by the Amsterdam Draft Treaty. Another example for variable geometry is the West European Union (WEU), of which only ten of the present EU countries are members.

	Multi-speed Europe	Concentric circles	Core Europe	Europe à *la carte*	Flexible integration	Closer cooperation
Strategy to solve deepening–widening dilemma	Parallel deepening and widening	Gradual integration	Parallel deepening and widening	Widening	Parallel deepening	Parallel deepening and widening
End product of integration/ theoretical approach	Supranational state/ Federalism	2/3 layers of different degrees of unification/ federalism	Supranational state/Federalism	Free trade area/ Intergovernmentalism	Supranational common base and intergovernmental open partnerships	Political union/ 'Federalism'
Instrument (variable) of differentiation	Time	Geographical, functional and temporal differentiation	Functional differentiation ('matter')	Functional differentiation ('matter')	Functional differentiation ('matter')	Functional differentiation ('matter')
Reason for differentiation	Objective lack of ability to deepen	Lacking ability and will to deepen	Lacking political will of non-core MS to deepen	Lacking political will to deepen	Lacking political will to deepen	Lacking political will of few MS to deepen
Maintenance of a common framework	Yes	Yes	Yes, but new institutions for the core	If yes, only a minimal common base	Yes, but restriction of EU power to economic (and related) issues	Yes
Examples	EMS, EMU	EU-EFTA-CEEC	–	EMU, CFSP	EMU	JHA after Amsterdam

Figure 3.1

4

The Debate on Differentiated Integration in the Context of the 1996 IGC and the Flexibility Clause of the Treaty of Amsterdam

The brief discussion of six alternative methods of European integration has revealed that they differ considerably in terms of the method of differentiation, the assumptions on the process of European integration and the end product of integration. Indeed, Stubb has discovered three main variables of differentiation: time, space and matter (Stubb 1995). Behind these methodological differences lie different assumptions concerning the directionality of European integration and the role intra-EU heterogeneity plays in this process. Multi-speed Europe, for instance, regards the increasing political heterogeneity of EU member states as a less important obstacle to deepening than economic differences. It assumes that the definition of common goals is still possible and desired by all countries: weaker member states only have to be given more time than stronger countries to implement the agreed measures. Multi-speed Europe thus maintains the original idea of an ever closer union. In complete opposition to multi-speed Europe, the functional concepts of Europe *à la carte* and variable geometry assume that increasing diversification of national interests regarding European integration makes it impossible to define common goals. They therefore promote an integration process in which member states build alliances around areas of equal interest. Both concepts thus tend to turn the EU into a purely intergovernmental (free trade) organisation. Core Europe and flexible integration are attempts to preserve some elements of supranationalism while at the same time considering the centrifugal effects of enlargement – core Europe by assuming a natural homogeneity of the founding members, flexible integration by defining a common base.

Multi-speed and core Europe thus also differ from the functional concepts by assuming the existence of 'higher' motivations for European integration in addition to mainly utilitarian ones.

These differences are not only of analytical value but also offer a framework against which the flexibility clause of the Amsterdam Treaty can be judged. However, in order to be able to do this, its emergence and context must be discussed. The following paragraphs will therefore first highlight the political debate on flexibility in the context of the 1996 IGC and then examine the provisions on flexibility in the Treaty of Amsterdam.

THE POLITICAL DEBATE ON DIFFERENTIATED INTEGRATION

The debate on differentiated integration takes place essentially on two levels: in academic and political circles. The academic debate on differentiated integration of the mid-1990s 'obviously arose as a response to the political debate' (Stubb 1997 p42). Political scientists and students of law were mostly concerned with defining and categorising the multitude of concepts in discussion. In doing so, academics filled the gap in quality literature on the subject that had existed since the 1970s (Stubb 1997 pp40–1). The academic debate on differentiated integration was thus mostly analytical and left normative questions to European politicians.

The political debate in the years preceding the 1996 IGC, on the other hand, was predominantly normative–practical and revolved around the appropriate strategy of differentiated integration to be taken and the conditions to be obeyed. According to Stubb (1997 pp42–3), there are essentially two reasons why the political debate on differentiated integration emerged. The prospect of eastern enlargement and the inefficient functioning of the second and third pillars is the first, and more straightforward reason. As pointed out in Chapter 1, the ever increasing cultural and political heterogeneity of EU member states, rather than economic disparities, demands the introduction of alternative concepts of integration. Second, flexibility could be regarded as a response to unanimous decision making:

> *Constructive abstention stands somewhere between unanimity and qualified majority voting. It is a way in which to seek a compromise between the two forms of decision-making: if a decision is blocked, the willing and able member states would be able to proceed (Stubb 1997 pp42–3).*

Differentiated integration has thus emerged as a response to tensions between integrationist and intergovernmentalist member states.

The issue of differentiated integration was put on the agenda of the 1996 IGC as a consequence of the initiatives of Lamers, Schäuble, Balladur and Major in 1994 (Stubb 1997 p42) in addition to the issues explicitly foreseen for revision in the TEU (extension of the application of the codecision procedure, security and defence, energy, tourism and civil protection, hierarchy of Community acts). On 29 March 1996 the European Council of Turin formally asked the IGC of the EU to

> *examine whether and how to introduce rules either of a general nature or in specific areas in order to enable a certain number of Member States to develop strengthened co-operation, open to all, compatible with the Union's objectives, while preserving the* acquis communautaire, *avoiding discrimination and distortions of competition and respecting the single institutional framework (quoted in Stubb 1997 p37).*

Thus, before and during the 1996 IGC the member states prepared documents that outlined their position on differentiated integration. The predominant characteristic of this political debate was that some form of differentiated integration in the EU framework was accepted by most member states, if sometimes only reluctantly. For instance, the Belgian submission to the IGC, which was later adopted as a joint memorandum on the IGC by all Benelux countries, lays down that 'it would be unacceptable for one or more Member States to be allowed to hold up progress on European integration towards an ever closer union among the peoples of Europe' (quoted in Federal Trust 1996). Similar opinions can also be found in the statements of, for instance, the French, German and Spanish governments (Intergovernmental Conference Briefing (ICB) no. 4/38, third update, 1996). Some countries (such as the Benelux countries, France and Sweden) stressed, however, that they regard differentiated integration only as a means of last resort, ie as a means to prevent stagnation of the European integration process due to national vetoes. Denmark, Finland, Greece and Ireland were probably most sceptical about the introduction of differentiated integration. In their documents put forward at the 1996 IGC the governments of the respective member states expressed strong concern about the potentially negative effects of differentiated integration on the EU, especially about the possible rise of two-/multi-class member states (ICB pp8–9).

Despite certain differences of attitudes EU member states share the following convictions concerning differentiated integration (ICB):

- Most member states regard multi-speed Europe as an acceptable mode of integration. There are several likely explanations for this phenomenon. Multi-speed Europe has been tested as a method of European integration and proved worthwhile. Moreover, its application does not demand a reform of the Community's political system or a debate about the *finalité* of European integration. Yet the approach has some potential for the solution to the problem of deepening and widening. Multi-speed Europe thus corresponds well to the pragmatic character of European integration.
- All member states, possibly except Britain, reject Europe *à la carte.* Europe *à la carte* rejects major principles of European integration, above all the progression of all member states towards an ever closer union and solidarity. Instead, the concept regards the value of national interests as absolute. In particular, the founding countries reject such a utilitarian approach to European integration which risks turning the EU into an intergovernmental organisation.
- Most member states reject the creation of a hard core of countries that would be closed to further members. Most countries were not only unhappy about the rather arbitrary selection of the core countries in the Lamers/Schäuble paper, but also about the creation of a two-class Community that would bar them from participation in policies whose communitarisation might be in their national interest. Generally:

> *[t]he division concerning variable geometry, ie the institutionalisation of a general flexibility clause into the Treaties, illustrates a surprising coalition between the three newest member states and the founding six members: France, Germany, the Benelux countries, Italy, Finland, Sweden (some reservations) and Austria seem willing to pursue variable solutions which do not necessarily incorporate all member states as long as strict principles managing flexibility are established (Stubb 1997 p42).*

As well as accepting the necessity of some form of differentiation, most member states also believe that certain rules have to be obeyed in order to make differentiated integration viable. All member states seemed to agree on the following conditions:

- Maintenance of the *acquis communautaire*. Differentiated integration must not jeopardise the present *acquis communautaire*. It may only be used in order to advance with European integration, the present degree of integration may not be reversed.
- Single institutional framework. Differentiated integration is to be managed by the existing institutions; no additional institutions are to be created by vanguard member states. While this rule aims at maintaining institutional transparency it evokes procedural questions, especially concerning the participation of the slower countries in the decision-making process.
- Openness. Willing and able member states must not be excluded from participation in arrangements of differentiated integration; opting in must be possible. With this rule the creation of a closed core of countries that pursue closer cooperation among themselves is prevented.
- Differentiated integration is to remain the exception rather than the rule. Differentiated integration is only

to be used as a means of last resort and 'only after all other options have been exhausted' (Stubb 1997 p50).

- Minimum participation. A minimum number of member states should participate in arrangements of differentiated integration.

Other questions debated in the course of the IGC concerned the voting procedure to start differentiated integration, the duration of respective arrangements, the financing of both the common base and enhanced cooperations and the roles of the Commission and ECJ (Stubb 1997, p50).

While all member states thus favour more flexibility in the process of European integration, these restrictions proposed by the member states clearly reflect a determination to avoid the creation of Europe *à la carte* or core Europe. They are targeted at maintaining as far as possible the present structure of the Union and thus suggest a certain wariness as regards the consequences of differentiation for the process of European integration.

As we will see in the following section, most of these conditions have found their way into the flexibility clause of the Treaty of Amsterdam.

THE FLEXIBILITY CLAUSE OF THE TREATY OF AMSTERDAM

The provisions on flexibility in the Treaty of Amsterdam permit a majority of member states to enter into closer cooperation in two pillars of the EU while maintaining the present institutional and legal framework. Provisions on flexibility are found in several parts of the Treaty and are divided into general clauses and specific clauses. The general provisions on flexibility are found in Title A 'General clauses to be inserted as a new title in the common provisions of the TEU' of Section V *Closer Cooperation – 'Flexibility'*. The specific provisions, which regulate the application of flexibility in the first and third pillar, are found in Title V B 'Clauses specific to the TEC' and Article K.12. Due to strong opposition by some member states no specific provisions on flexibility in the CFSP were inserted in the Treaty.

The *general clauses*, which will be inserted as Title VI A in the TEU, apply therefore only to the first and third pillars of the EU, not to the second pillar. They permit able and willing member states to establish closer cooperation between themselves. In order to prevent the EU from becoming fragmented institutionally and politically a set of conditions has to be obeyed before and after the establishment of closer cooperation. The eight conditions laid down in Article A 1 of the Treaty of Amsterdam can be divided into two groups. Some refer to the EU and aim at preserving its present political and institutional framework. The Treaty determines that closer cooperation must be 'aimed at furthering the objectives of the Union and at protecting and serving its interests' (1a) and must not 'affect the "acquis communautaire" and the measures adopted under the other provisions of the Treaties' (1e). Both provisions have been laid down in order to ensure that member states only use the instrument of 'closer cooperation' in order to advance European integration, and not to reverse decisions already achieved (Ehlermann 1998 pp 9–10). In addition, the institutional framework of the EU has to be maintained. Article 1b rules that 'the principles of the Treaties and the single institutional framework of the Union must be respected'. Member states entering into closer cooperation may thus not establish a new, separate, set of institutions, but have to make use of the existing ones.

The other provisions of Article A 1 refer specifically to flexibility and lay down the rules of application for enhanced cooperation. On the one hand they target the problem of opacity inherent in all arrangements of differentiated integration by greatly restricting the use of enhanced cooperation. The instrument may only be applied if it is a means of last resort (1c) and concerns at least a majority of member states (1d). Due to these conditions closer cooperation will not be easy to apply: even if in one area no compromise solution can be found the increasing size of the Union will make it harder to find a majority of member states for the establishment of enhanced cooperation. On the other hand, the relationship between 'open partnerships' and 'common base' is addressed. Flexibility must not have negative effects of any kind on non-participating member states (1f) and has to be open to all countries (1g). In addition, the application of closer cooperation must also comply with the specific additional criteria laid down in Article 5a of the TEC (1f).

In order to prevent the creation of 'closed clubs' Article A 2 determines that *all* EU member states have the right to participate in the deliberations on the establishment of the cooperation. However, only those member states that participate in the cooperation are allowed to take part in the decision taking. Once the cooperation is set up decisions are taken according to the institutional provisions laid down for the respective policy area in the TEU.

The *clauses specific to the TEC*, the new Article 5a TEC, determine not only the conditions for application of closer cooperation in the first pillar but also participation of the institutions in a more detailed fashion than the general clauses.

According to the prospective Article 5a TEC closer cooperation may be established if it does not concern areas that fall within the exclusive competence of the Community (1a), does not affect Community policies, actions or programmes (1b), does not concern the citizenship of the Union or discriminate between nationals of member states (1c), remains within the limits of the powers conferred upon the Community by the Treaty (1d) and does not constitute a discrimination or a restriction of trade between member states and does not distort the conditions of competition between the latter (1e). The main practical effect of these conditions is to greatly restrict the applicability of closer cooperation. Article 1a excludes large policy areas from closer cooperation so that the first pillar 'offers the least opportunity for closer cooperation' (Ehlermann 1998 p13). Article 1d prevents member states from integrating policies that are not part of the *acquis communautaire*.

In order to be able to create a circle of closer cooperation interested countries have to address a request to the Commission. The Commission then submits a proposal to the Council, which has to be adopted by qualified majority after consultation of the European Parliament (Article 5a (2) first and third subparagraph). However, a vote is not taken if 'a member of the Council declares that, for important and stated reasons of national policy, it intends to oppose the granting of an authorisation by qualified majority'. Instead, the Council may then decide by qualified majority to refer the matter to the European Council for a decision by unanimity (Article 5a (2) second subparagraph). If a member state intends to join a cooperation it must inform the Council and the Commission. The Commission, after having passed on an opinion to the Council, then decides on the application within four months of the date of the notification (Article 5a (3)).

According to Article K.12 closer cooperation may also be established in the third pillar if it aims at enabling the Union to develop more rapidly into an area of freedom, security and justice (Article K.12 (1a)). In general, the initiation procedure is similar to the one in the first pillar. In correspondence with the intergovernmental character of JHA, however, the Commission has less power than it does in the EC. The Commission is merely 'invited to present its opinion' before the Council decides (by qualified majority) on the authorisation of closer cooperation in the third pillar. Equally, it is the Council that decides about the application of a member state to participate in an established cooperation. The Commission has only the right to give an opinion on the application.

The essence of closer cooperation as laid down in the Treaty of Amsterdam can thus be summarised as follows. The present *acquis communautaire* constitutes both the minimum requirement of EU membership and the framework that may not be exceeded by initiatives of closer cooperation. Within this framework, those policies that fall within the exclusive competence of the Community are excluded from differentiation (eg CAP, the structural funds, trade policy). They therefore constitute the common base. Policies of the first and third pillar that are not part of this common base are available for differentiated integration in the form of open partnerships. This means that a majority of member states can create a circle of closer cooperation in these fields as long as the remaining countries are given the possibility to enter once they are able and willing to.

On the basis of this summary closer cooperation can be categorised easily and thus put in relation to the concepts of differentiated integration introduced above. Closer cooperation belongs to the group of functional concepts of differentiated integration. It recognises that due to continuous enlargement member state ideas regarding the desirable character and *finalité politique* of the EU differ increasingly so that common goals can become difficult to define. Unlike in the past, when multi-speed solutions were sought and opt outs were regarded as unique exemptions, not only temporarily but, if necessary, also permanently, different degrees of integration are now accepted. The flexibility clauses of the Treaty of Amsterdam thus constitute a remarkable step away from uniform integration that only six years ago was categorically rejected by most member states. At the same time, however, measures have been taken to avoid the emergence of both Europe *à la carte* and core Europe, concepts that were opposed by most member states during the 1996 IGC. The exclusion of wide policy areas from differentiated integration and the requirement that only a majority of member states can establish a circle of closer cooperation effectively prevents *à la carte* integration or core Europe. Indeed, as indicated by the terminology used above, the structure of closer cooperation resembles most that of flexible integration. Although modified to suit the practical requirements of European integration, the main elements of the two concepts are very similar.

While the inclusion of the flexibility clause has laid the foundation for reconciling the tasks of deepening and widening, the great restrictions in its application raise questions concerning the usefulness of the instrument. Indeed, they confirm the conclusion drawn above that, although flexibility has been included in the Treaty of Amsterdam, the idea of differentiated integration is only embraced reluctantly by the member states.

Janning (1997 p286) argues that closer cooperation was subjected to 'strict normative limits and procedural fetters that are only little below the threshold of uselessness of the instrument'. Two provisions seem particularly problematic. First, the condition that only a *majority* of member states may establish closer cooperation between themselves is in fundamental contrast to the original idea of flexibility: to enable countries with similar interests to continue with deepening despite a rising number of member states.

> *Those member states that have a high convergence in, for example, the areas of social and environmental policies, in the fiscal policy or in the security and defence policy do not form a majority in the respective areas. In that sense flexibility becomes less practical with a rising number of member states (Janning 1997 p289).*

Second, although the decision on the establishment of a circle of closer cooperation is taken by majority vote, it can be vetoed by one single member state 'for important and stated reasons of national policy' (Article 5 a (2)). The actual creation of closer cooperation thus *de facto* depends on one member state only. Not least due to this provision the actual application of the flexibility clause could be rather restrained in future EU policies.

These limits of closer cooperation prevent a full exploitation of its potential assets. They are aimed at preserving the present character of European integration to the greatest extent possible and emphasise the fact that flexibility is considered, and laid down, as an instrument of last resort. The provisions on closer cooperation in the Treaty of Amsterdam represent, however, the difference between the idealism of a theoretical concept and political realities. The flexibility clause of the Treaty of Amsterdam thus constitutes only a first step away from the paradigm of uniform integration. The decisive progress consists not so much in the content of the respective articles but in their mere inclusion in the Treaty.

5

Summary and Conclusion

At the beginning of this Dossier it was argued that with the last enlargement a threshold has been reached so that the classical Community method of widening will become impractical. While in the past widening entailed merely the extension of the *acquis communautaire* to the new member states and superficial adaptation on the side of the EU, future enlargement will also demand comprehensive reform of the Union itself. This close interrelation between deepening and widening is, however, problematic, since it poses a dilemma that is unsolvable in the present, and above all, future EU. The Union has been founded as an economic organisation and, although its founding fathers also had a political vision, from the outside it has long been perceived merely as an intergovernmentalist and economic construct. Continuous widening could (and will) thus add to the rather homogeneous founding countries member states with a wide variety of attitudes towards the character and goal of European integration that are based on different historical traditions and geopolitical reasoning. The increasing political and economic heterogeneity among member states constitutes the greatest obstacle to the required deepening of the EU.

The prospect of an eastern enlargement that could bring up to ten more countries into the EU exposes the limits of the uniform mode of integration that is based on political and economic homogeneity among member states. Although this is not the cause of the anticipated difficulties it will exacerbate them to a critical extent. Indeed, the limits of uniform integration had already become obvious after the first enlargement. Consequently, forms of differentiation were found that were applied within the framework of uniformity: transition periods following the inclusion of new member states, implementation of regulations in a manner that reflects particular national circumstances, a multi-speed EMU and the opt outs negotiated at Maastricht are, among others, examples of this differentiation within uniformity.

The modes of differentiation hitherto applied have, however, been commonly regarded as merely irritating requirements and unique exemptions to the dogma of uniform progression. This began to change in the years preceding the 1996 IGC when both academics and politicians started to discuss strategies of differentiated integration as serious alternatives to uniform integration and thus were responsible for the renaissance of concepts often 30 years old. The academic contribution to the discussion was mostly analytical: old and new approaches were defined and categorised, thus reducing some of the mystery surrounding differentiated integration. However, it is also obvious that for the time being most of the concepts introduced above will only serve as role models for differentiation in political practice. A fast introduction of particularly the functional concepts Europe *à la carte*, variable geometry, flexible integration and core Europe would demand too radical changes to the present system in order to be viable. Their application would also create organisational problems that would be difficult to solve (eg the relation of the various functional circles to each other). Most importantly, however, the adoption of one of these 'pure' concepts might even make deepening more difficult. First, there is a strong argument that 'spill-over processes ... in a world of sectoral interdependences reduce any separation of policy fields to artificial and inefficient solutions' (Wessels 1993 p36). In contrast to the assumptions of functional concepts, progress in European integration has always been 'based on a dynamic "mix of policy areas"' (Wessels 1993 p36), exemplified by the adoption of the so-called package deals. A separation of policies in different sectors could thus rather lead to regression than progress in deepening. Second, the role of the supranational institutions would invariably be smaller. As we have shown above, however, both Commission and ECJ have played an important role in shaping the present Union beyond the intentions of the member states. A loss of their influence would mean losing influential advocates and actors for the cause of deepening.

Against this background the pragmatic flexibility clauses of the Treaty of Amsterdam do have the advantage of leaving the institutional structure of the EU largely unchanged and providing for a comprehensive participation of the institutions in the decisions on closer cooperation. At the same time they also allow for more flexibility in the process of European integration.

However, it is also clear that closer cooperation in its present form can only mark the beginning of the institutionalisation of differentiation in the Treaties. Given the increasing tension between deepening and widening, differentiation will gain in importance in the European integration process. In order to be able to fulfil its increasingly important role closer cooperation will have to be reformed, possibly in the direction of flexible integration. While the disintegrative forces of a less restrictive flexibility clause are obvious, it will become necessary at least to abandon the majority requirement and the national veto. This will make closer cooperation much easier to apply and thus create a basis on which the instrument can fully develop its advantages over uniform integration. In the longer run a clearer definition of the common base and an extension of areas of application will be required.

If reforms in this direction are successfully introduced the new flexibility clauses will become a viable instrument to counter the disintegrative forces of the ever greater political heterogeneity of the EU and to ensure that the progression towards an ever closer union of at least a few member states continues to be possible.

References

Baldwin, R. E. (1994) *Towards an Integrated Europe*, Centre for Economic Policy Research

Bideleux, R. (1996) 'The Southern enlargement of the EC. Greece, Portugal and Spain', in R. Bideleux and R. Taylor *European Integration and Disintegration. East and West*, Routledge: London

Borsámyi, G, Hauszmann, J. and Kurtán, S. (1996) 'Zwischen zwei Ufern: Wandlungen des ungarischen Europabildes', Bundeszentrale für politische Bildung (ed.) *Europabilder in Mittel- und Osteuropa*

Brandt, Willy (1975) 'Rede des Vorsitzenden der Sozialdemokratischen Partei Deutschlands vor der Organisation Française du Mouvement Européen, Paris, 19 November 1974 (Auszüge), printed in *Europa-Archiv*, 33 (2)

Centre for Economic Policy Research (1995) *Flexible Integration. Towards a More Effective and Democratic Europe*, Centre for Economic Policy Research

Chaltiel, F. (1995) 'Pour une clarification du débat sur l'Europe à plusieurs vitesses' *Revue du Marché commun et de l'Union européenne*, No. 384, January

Commissariat Général du Plan (1980) L´Europe les vingt prochaines années, Paris 1980

Commission of the European Communities (1976) 'European Union. Report by Mr Leo Tindemans, Prime Minister of Belgium, to the European Council', *Bulletin of the European Communities,* Supplement 1/76

Cram, L. (1994) 'The European Commission as a multi-organisation: social policy and IT policy in the EU' *Journal of European Public Policy*, 1 (2)

da Silva Lopes, J. (1993) *Portugal and EC Membership Evaluated*, Pinter: London

Deubner, Ch. (1995) *Deutsche Europapolitik: Von Maastricht nach Kerneuropa?*, Nomos Verlagsgesellschaft: Baden-Baden

Ehlermann, C.-D. (1998) *Differentiation, Flexibility, Closer Cooperation: The New Provisions of the Amsterdam Treaty*, EUI Working Paper

Europäische Kommission *Agenda 2000. Eine stärkere und erweiterte Union*, Bulletin der Europäischen Union. Beilage 5/97

Eurostat (1996) *1996 Begegnung in Zahlen. Ein statistisches Porträt der Europäischen Union*, Luxemburg

Federal Trust (1996) *Federal Trust Conference 11 June 1996: Dividing the Union? Britain and the IGC*, Background paper, 22 May, http://europa.eu.int/en/agenda/igc-home/instdoc/universe/fedtrust.htm

Financial Times (1998) *Survey*, 'Investing in Central and Eastern Europe' 8 May

Giering, C. (1997) 'Vertiefung durch Differenzierung – Flexibilisierungskonzepte in der aktuellen Reformdebatte' *Integration*, 20 (2)

Grabbe, H. and K. Hughes (1997) *Eastward Enlargement of the European Union*, Royal Institute of International Affairs, European Programme

Holman, O. (1996) *Integrating Southern Europe. EC Expansion and the Transnationalization of Spain*, Routledge: London

Holzer, J. (1996) 'Polen in Europa: Zentrum oder Peripherie?', in Bundeszentrale fur politische Bildung (ed.) *Europabilder in Mittel- und Osteuropa*

Intergovernmental Conference *Briefing no. 4: Differentiated Integration* (third update), http://www.europarl.eu.int/dg7/fiches/en/fiche/1.htm

Janning, J. (1997) 'Dynamik in der Zwangsjacke – Flexibilität in der Europäischen Union nach Amsterdam' *Integration*, 20 (4) (author's translation)

Lamers, K. (1997) 'Strengthening the Hard Core', in P. Gowan and P. Anderson (eds) *The Question of Europe*, Verso: London

Langeheine, B. and U. Weinstock (1984) 'Graduated Integration: A Modest Path Towards Progress' *Journal of Common Market Studies*, 23 (2) December

Mazconkai (1996) in F. Madl and P. Mueller-Graff (eds) *Hungary – From Europe Agreement to a Member Status in the European Union*, Nomos Verlagsgesellschaft, Baden Baden

Miles, L. (1995) 'The European Union and the Nordic Countries: Impacts on the Integration Process', in C. Rhodes and S. Mazey (eds) *The State of the European Union Vol. 3: Building a European Polity?* Lynne Reinner Publishers

Moorhouse, J. (1996) 'Ostmitteleuropa auf dem Weg in die Europäische Union' *Aussenpolitik*, IV

Nugent, N. (1992) 'The Deepening and Widening of the European Community: Recent Evolution, Maastricht, and Beyond' *Journal of Common Market Studies*, 30 (3) September

Pinder, J. (1992) 'The Future of the European Community: A Strategy for Enlargement' *Government and Opposition*, 27 (4)

Preston, Ch. (1995) 'Obstacles to EU enlargement: The Classical Community Method and the Prospects for a Wider Europe' *Journal of Common Market Studies*, 33 (3) September

Samson, I. (1996) 'Die Slowakei: Grenze zwischen Ost und West', in Bundeszentrale für politische Bildung (ed) *Europabilder in Mittel- und Osteuropa*

Scharrer, H.-E. (1984) 'Abgestufte Integration – Eine Einführung', in E. Grabitz (ed) *Abgestufte Integration: eine Alternative zum herkömmlichen Integrationskonzept?*, N.P. Engel Verlag

Stercken, H. (ed) (1969) *Vive la France - Vive l´Europe! Aus den Reden Charles de Gaulles 1958–1968*: Munich

Stubb, A. C-G. (1995) *The Semantic Indigestion of Differentiated Integration*, College of Europe: Bruges, p.19

Stubb, A. C-G. (1997) 'The 1996 Intergovernmental Conference and the management of flexible integration' *Journal of European Public Policy*, 4 (1) March

Thatcher, M. (1988) *Britain and Europe:* Text of Speech Delivered in Bruges by the Prime Minister on 20 September, London: Conservative Political Centre, p.4

Timmermann, H. (1993) 'Europa - der zentrale Bezugspunkt für die Länder des Ostens. Erwartungen, Möglichkeiten, Konzeptionen' *Osteuropa*, Vol. 43, August

'Überlegungen zur europäischen Politik' (1994) Positionspapier der CDU/CSU-Bundestagsfraktion vom 1 September, printed in *Blätter für deutsche und internationale Politik*, No. 10

Wessels, W. (1993) 'Deepening versus Widening? Debate on the Shape of EC-Europe in the Nineties', in W. Wessels and Ch. Engel (eds) *The European Union in the 1990s - Ever closer and larger?*, Europa Union Verlag

Wincott, D. (1995) 'The role of law or the rule of the Court of Justice? An "institutional" account of judicial politics in the European Community' *Journal of European Public Policy*, 2 (4)

Bibliography

PRIMARY SOURCE MATERIAL

Commission Européen (1997) *Historique de la conférence intergouvernementale 1996*, 9 October, http://europa.eu.int/en/agenda/igc-home/eu-doc/commissn/notefin2.htm

Commission of the European Communities (1997) *Agenda 2000 – Summary and Conclusions of the Opinions of Commission concerning the Applications for Membership to the European Union, presented by the candidate countries*, July, DOC/97/8

Commission of the European Communities (1996) *Commission Opinion Reinforcing Political Union and Preparing for Enlargement*, 28 February, http://europa.eu.int/

Commission of the European Communities *Europe and the Challenge of Enlargement*, Bulletin of the European Communities. Supplement 3/92

Draft Treaty of Amsterdam (1997) August (http://ue.eu.int/Amsterdam/en/treaty/)

Europäische Kommission (1997) 'Der Vertrag von Amsterdam. Ergebnisse, Erläuterungen, Vertragsentwurf' *EU-Nachrichten Dokumentation*, 3 (3) July

European Commission (1997) *Background Report. The Enlargement of the European Union*, February

European Commission (1996) *Eurobarometer. Public Opinion in the European Union*, No. 44, spring

European Commission (1995a) *Eurobarometer. Public Opinion in the European Union*, No. 43, autumn

European Commission (1995b) *Central and Eastern Eurobarometer*, No. 5, March

European Commission (1992) *Eurobarometer. Public Opinion in the European Union*, Trends 1974–1992

Eurostat (1996) *Yearbook '96. A Statistical View on Europe 1985–1995*, Luxembourg

Hallet, M. (1997) *National and Regional Development in Central and Eastern Europe: Implications for EU Structural Assistance*, Directorate General for Economic and Financial Affairs: Economic Papers, No. 120, March

Intergovernmental Conference (1997) *Briefing no. 4: Differentiated Integration* (fourth update: 19 March), http://www.europarl.eu.int/dg7/fiches/en/fiche/4.htm

Intergovernmental Conference *Briefing no. 25: The 1996 IGC and the effectiveness of the Union* (second update), http://www.europarl.eu.int/dg7/fiche 25.htm#f2

Trans European Policy Studies Association (1992) *Enlarged Community: Institutional Adaptation*, European Parliament (Directorate General for Research), Working Papers: Political Series 17, Brussels/Bonn

SECONDARY SOURCES

Books

Baun, M. J. (1996) *An Imperfect Union. The Maastricht Treaty and the New Politics of European Integration*, Westview Press Inc.

Bideleux, R. and R. Taylor (1996) *European Integration and Disintegration. East and West*, Routledge: London

Bundeszentrale für politische Bildung (ed) (1996) *Europabilder in Mittel-und Osteuropa. Neue Herausforderungen für die politische Bildung*, Bonn

Francioni, F. (ed) (1992) *Italy and EC Membership evaluated*, Pinter: London

Gowan, P. and P. Anderson (eds) (1997) *The Question of Europe*, Verso: London

Grabitz, E. (ed) (1984) *Abgestufte Integration: eine Alternative zum herkömmlichen Integrationskonzept?*, N. P. Engel Verlag

Ludlow P. *et al.* (1996) *Preparing for Membership. The Eastward and Southern Enlargement of the EU*, Centre for European Policy Studies

Mádl, F. and P.-Ch. Müller-Graff (eds) (1996) *Hungary – From Europe Agreement to a Member Status in the European Union*, Nomos Verlagsgesellschaft: Baden-Baden

Mayer, O. G. and H.-E. Scharrer (eds) (1997) *Osterweiterung der Europäischen Union. Sind die mittel- und osteuropäischen Länder und die EU reif für eine Erweiterung?*, Nomos Verlagsgesellschaft: Baden-Baden

Michalski, A. and H. Wallace (1992) *The European Community: The Challenge of Enlargement*, Royal Institute of International Affairs: London

Newman, M. (1996) *Democracy, Sovereignty and the European Union*, Hurst: London

O'Neill, M. (1996) *The Politics of European Integration*, Routledge: London

Redmond, J. and G. G. Rosenthal (eds) (1998) *The Expanding European Union. Past, Present and Future*, Lynne Rienner Publishers

Redmond, J. (ed) (1998) *Prospective Europeans. New Members for the European Union*, Harvester Wheatsheaf: Hemel Hempstead

Rhodes, C. and S. Mazey (1995) *The State of the European Union. Vol. 3: Building a European Polity?*, Lynne Rienner Publishers

Wallace, H. (1995) *Europe: The Challenge of Diversity*, Royal Institute of International Affairs: London

Wallace H. and W. Wallace (eds) (1996) *Policy-Making in the European Union*, Oxford University Press

Weidenfeld, W. (ed) (1995) *Demokratie und Marktwirtschaft in Osteuropa. Strategien für Europa*, Bundeszentrale für politische Bildung

Weidenfeld, W. and W. Wessels (eds) (1995) *Europa von A-Z. Taschenbuch der Europäischen Integration*, Europa Union Verlag

Wessels, W. and Ch. Engel (eds) (1993) *The European Union in the 1990s – Ever closer and larger?*, Europa Union Verlag

Articles

Bieber, R. (1997) 'Reformen der Institutionen und Verfahren – Amsterdam kein Meisterstück' *Integration*, 20 (4)

Bousfield, A. (1996) 'The Problems of European Integration: A Study of the Failure to Develop a European Civic Nationalism' (unpublished)

Brok, E. (1997) 'Der Amsterdamer Vertrag: Etappe auf dem Weg zur europäischen Einigung' *Integration*, 20 (4)

Carey, M. (1997) 'In at any price' *Europ*, No. 86, summer

Cremona, M. (1994) 'The "Dynamic and Homogenous" EEA: Byzantine Structures and Variable Geometry' *European Law Review*, 19, October

Dauderstädt, M. and B. Lippert (1996) 'No Integration without Differentiation', Friedrich-Ebert-Stiftung, February, http://www-fes.gmd.de/organisation/europe/daumsd.html

Davey, W. J. (1995) 'European Integration: Reflection on its Limits and Effects' *Indiana Global Legal Studies Journal*, 1, http://www.law.indiana.edu

The Economist (1997) 'A budget for reform', 19 July

The Economist (1997) 'Eastward ho, they said warily', 19 July

The Economist (1997) 'Welcome to Europe' 19 July

Editorial comments 'The Treaty of Amsterdam: Neither a bang nor a whimper' *Common Market Law Review*, 34 (4) August 1997

Edwards, G. and G. Wiessala (1998) 'Editorial: Flexibility, Legitimacy and Identity in Post-Amsterdam Europe' *Journal of Common Market Studies*, 36, Annual Review. September

George, S. (1996) 'The approach of the British government to the 1996 Intergovernmental Conference of the European Union' *Journal of European Public Policy*, 3 (1) March

Hirst, P. (1994) 'Security Challenges in Post-Communist Europe' *The Political Quarterly*, Supplement: Military Intervention in European Conflicts

Holtbrügge, D. (1996) 'Ökonomische Voraussetzungen und Folgen einer Osterweiterung der Europäischen Union' *Osteuropa*

Huldt, B. (1996) 'Schweden und die Europäische Union' *Aus Politik und Zeitgeschichte*, B10, March

Karppinen, A. (1996) 'Finland in der Europäischen Union' *Aus Politik und Zeitgeschichte*, B10, March 1996

Lipsius, J. (1995) 'The 1996 Intergovernmental Conference' *European Law Review*, 20, February

Maillet, P. (1995) 'Convergence et géométrie variable. L'organisation du fonctionnement de l'Union européenne diversifiée est à repenser' *Revue du Marché commun et de l'Union européenne*, No. 386, March

Möschel, W. (1995) 'Europapolitik zwischen deutscher Romantik und gallischer Klarheit' *Aus Politik und Zeitgeschichte*, B3-4, January

Müller-Brandeck-Brocquet, G. (1997) 'Der Amsterdamer Vertrag zur Reform der Europäischen Union. Ergebnisse, Fortschritte, Defizite' *Aus Politik und Zeitgeschichte*, B 47/97, 14 November

Nicoll, W. (1984) 'Paths to European Unity' *Journal of Common Market Studies*, 23 (2) December

Noetzold, J. (1995) 'European Union and Eastern Central Europe: Expectations and Uncertainties' *Aussenpolitik (German Foreign Affairs Review)*, 46 (1) 1st quarter

O'Keeffe, D. (1994) 'From Maastricht to the 1996 Intergovernmental Conference: The Challenges Facing the Union' *Legal Issues of European Integration*, No. 2

Pippan, Ch. (1997) 'Die Europäische Union nach Amsterdam: Stärkung ihrer Identität auf internationaler Ebene?' *Aus Politik und Zeitgeschichte*, B 47/97, 14 November

Rose, R. and Ch. Haerpfer (1995) 'Democracy and Enlarging the European Union Eastwards' *Journal of Common Market Studies*, 33 (3) September

Rupprecht, R. (1997) 'Justiz und Inneres nach dem Amsterdamer Vertrag' *Integration*, 20 (4)

Serre, F. de la (1996) 'L'élargissement aux PECO: quelle différenciation?' *Revue du Marché commun et de l'Union européenne*, No. 402, November

Sharpe, L.J. (1996) 'British Scepticism and the European Union. An Explanation', paper presented at the Disintegration in Europe Workshop, ECPR Joint Sessions, Oslo, April

Stubb, A. C-G. (1998) 'The Amsterdam Treaty and Flexible Integration' *European Community Studies Association (ECSA) Review*, 11 (2) spring

Timmermann, H. (1997) 'Osteuropa: "Drang nach Westen" – Möglichkeiten und Hemmnisse. Die Reformstaaten Mittel- und Osteuropas und die euro-atlantischen Integrationsprozesse' *Osteuropa*, Vol. 47, June

Timmins, Graham (1997) 'European Union policy towards east-central Europe: the prospects for enlargement' *Contemporary Politics*, 3 (1)

Ungerer, W. (1993) 'Institutional Consequences of Broadening and Deepening the Community: The Consequences for the Decision-making process' *Common Market Law Review*, 30

Usher, J. A. (1997) 'Variable Geometry or Concentric Circles: Patterns for the European Union' *International and Comparative Law Quarterly*, 46, Part 2, April

Wallace, H. (1997) 'Pan-European Integration: A Real or Imagined Community?' *Government and Opposition*, 32 (2) spring

Weidenfeld, W. *et al.* (1997) *Auf dem Weg nach Amsterdam – Europapolitische Essentials für die Reform der Europäischen Union*, Centrum für angewandte Politikforschung (CAP) der Ludwig-Maximilians-Universität München, May, http://www.lrz-muenchen.de

Pamphlets

Ehlermann, C.-D. *Increased Differentiation or Stronger Uniformity*, EUI Working Paper RSC No. 95/21

Maclay, M. (1992) *Multi-speed Europe? The Community Beyond Maastricht*, Royal Institute of International Affairs

Martin, P. (1994) *A Sequential Approach to Regional Integration: The European Union and Central and Eastern Europe*, Centre for Economic Policy Research: Discussion Paper Series No. 1070, November

Miles, L. (1995) *Enlargement of the European Union*, University of North London European Dossier Series No. 36

Noël, E. *La conférence intergouvernementale de 1996. Vers un nouvel ordre institutionnel*, EUI Working Paper RSC No. 95/22

Vibert, F. (1996) *Structured Flexibility in the European Union*, European Policy Forum, August

Appendix: Abbreviations

CAP	Common agricultural policy
CDU	Christlich-Demokratische Union (Christian-Democratic Union)
CSU	Christlich-Soziale Union (Christian-Social Union)
CEEC	Central and East European Countries
CFSP	Common Foreign and Security Policy
EBRD	European Bank for Reconstruction and Development
EC	European Community
ECJ	European Court of Justice
EEA	European Economic Area
EFTA	European Free Trade Area
EP	European Parliament
EMS	European Monetary System
EMU	Economic and Monetary Union
EU	European Union
GDP	Gross domestic product
IGC	Intergovernmental conference
JHA	Justice and Home Affairs
MEP	Member of the European Parliament
PU	Political union
SEA	Single European Act
SPD	Sozialdemokratische Partei Deutschlands (Social-Democratic Party of Germany)
TEC	Treaty on the European Community
TEU	Treaty on European Union
WEU	West European Union